Everything you need to know about Brand Partnerships

This book aims to be an in-depth guide on everything you need to know about Brand Partnerships — one of the fastest-growing marketing techniques of the 21st century.

Brand Partnerships are now widely recognised as a highly effective and engaging growth marketing technique for all businesses, from start-ups to global firms. Businesses agree that collaboration leads to growth and innovation. Spotify, Paypal, EasyJet and Uber are all taking advantage of the power of Brand Partnerships.

This book explains what Brand Partnerships are, and describes the many types, including a whole load of examples, as well as how to benefit from Brand Partnerships for your business.

Content: What this book will cover

We'll explore...

1. What are Brand Partnerships?
2. What are the 10 types of Brand Partnerships?
3. There are actually 3 core types!
4. Examples of Brand Partnerships
5. Difference between Affiliate Marketing and Brand Partnerships
6. How to decide which partners to work with

7. Why are Brand Partnerships are so lucrative yet so difficult for others? And how to succeed at them!

8. How to analyse a Brand Partnership both online and offline

Chapter 1: What are Brand Partnerships and what are the different types?

What are Brand Partnerships?

Brand Partnerships have in the past been described as Joint Marketing, Co-Marketing or Partnership Marketing, but we are now seeing *'Brand Partnerships'* or *'Partnership Marketing'* as the globally recognised terms.

Brand Partnerships have seen many definitions in recent years, but in its clearest form it should be described as:

"Where a brand has the ideal product or service to compliment another brand; utilising their target audiences to achieve their marketing objectives via partner campaigns and initiatives."

Chapter 2: 10 Types of Brand Partnerships

Below are the 10 types of Brand Partnerships — in no particular order. It should be said this is an ever-evolving practice. As technologies emerge we are seeing new types of partnerships appear every single year.

1. Affiliate Marketing

"Affiliate marketing is a performance marketing technique where websites otherwise known as publishers will promote your product or service in return for a monetary reward."

Affiliate Marketing can be achieved by using any of the methods described below. Both utilise a primary partner, often referred to as an advertiser, and a secondary partner, often referred to as the affiliate or the publisher. These partners work in collaboration; in doing so the primary brand benefits from promotion of their products resulting in sales (with some brand benefit), the secondary benefiting from commissions earned per lead or sale.

They are three ways brands can work with affiliates:

1. **In-House** – when a primary brand is looking for a solution that provides them with the ability to upload all creative banners, allow an affiliate to select the type of campaign with relevant tracking links and display all results in one centralised location, they use an affiliate program.
2. **Networks** – a third party where both advertiser and publisher register and utilise its services all through the network's external portal. A major benefit to brands over an in-house solution is that it provides far greater reach for

publishers to find relevant brands to promote, while the advertiser is immediately exposed to thousands of publisher sites rather than having to promote their own in-house programme.

3. **Agencies** – a third option is to work directly with an agency which manages the portfolio of affiliates as well as the operations behind it such as banners and tracking links. An agency can also be a network, or they can manage your own in-house solution, ultimately they should support your requirements in this channel.

Affiliates can promote an advertiser using numerous techniques. Depending on the type of website, unique selling point (USP), and target audience they will promote those with the highest conversion and those offering the greatest commission rates. Promotional formats include:

- **Banner ad** – banner ads are one of the more common forms of exposure for a partner brand on a publisher site.

Header (728×90) or Skyscraper (160×600) banners are most popular.

- **Text link** – a simple hyperlink often found within an article. It is more subtle than a banner ad.
- **Dedicated article** – a strong partnership between brands can lead to more unique forms of exposure. A dedicated article can engage a target audience and provide a more detailed product description than that of a text link or banner ad.
- **Promotional page** – exposure of advertisers through specific areas of the publisher's site devoted to promotional offers. Here promotional banner ads can be kept separate from the core content.
- **Newsletters** – for those affiliates that require accounts to be created or email addresses to be captured newsletters are a strategic way for them to directly market affiliate offers. Groupon and Quidco for example are excellent at targeting their segmented database with the latest partner deals.

- **Comparison table** – for aggregator sites such as Money.co.uk (below) and Confused.com, the comparison table is a huge USP, adds value, and attracts customers over other affiliates. It allows them to rank advertisers by pricing, features and benefits to consumers.

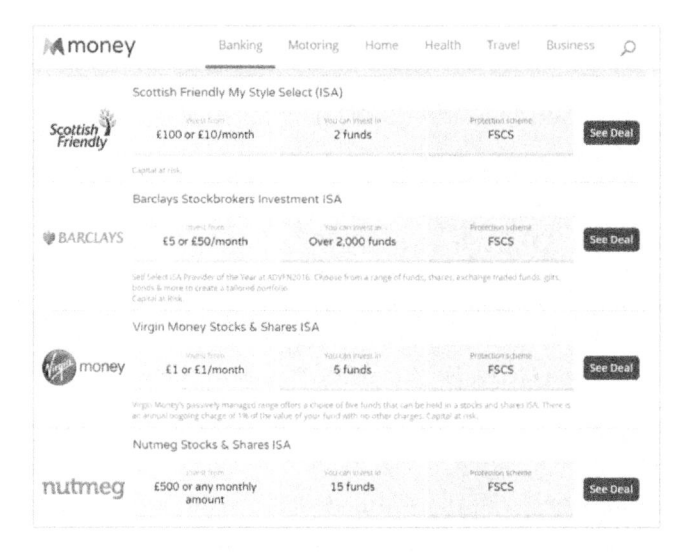

Example of Money.co.uk, a successful publisher that promotes other brands in their comparison table, in return for commission.

Affiliate marketing is widely considered to be one of the purest forms of Brand Partnership. It comes under the umbrella of performance marketing because it can be so accurately measured and the return on investment (ROI) precisely calculated. Affiliation is quantifiable and unlike some other marketing methods can always be proven.

Affiliation refers to the practice of partner websites promoting your brand in return for commissions. An affiliate will be paid depending on the agreement that has been made with the advertiser. It's not always a complete sale, there are many models that pay based on the number of impressions, clicks, or leads. This doesn't mean that an affiliate will always receive commissions on just one sale, the deal can be on multiples; CPM (cost per thousand impression), CPC (cost per click), CPA (cost per acquisition), revenue share (percentage of the revenue a sale generates), or a fixed fee per ad-spot. There are also amalgamations of these often referred to as hybrid deals.

An affiliate can range from a successful newspaper brand to a small niche one-man-band website reviewing headphones. Both of these follow the same principle as they contain content, attract traffic, and publish ads. There are a number of affiliate variants out there; voucher sites such as Groupon, cashback sites such as TopCashback, or comparison sites such as MoneySupermarket.com or Gocompare.

Bringing this back to Brand Partnerships; when primary brands are looking for specific partners to promote their services, affiliation is seen as a very attractive option. It creates an alliance of two brands in a very direct way towards a mutual target audience. LG for example, the popular TV manufacturer, will work closely with renowned TV review sites in order to drive sales. The review site will demonstrate the quality of the brand offering and effectively promote LG's products to their database.

2. Distribution Channels

"Where one partner agrees to cross-market or bundle another partner's product or services into their own distribution channels to target the agreed customer base."

There are two main types of distribution partnership, each a slightly different way to distribute a partner's product or service:

1. **Bundling** – including your partners offering as an in-box bundle or package insertion, such as giveaways in packaging, promotion within the product itself or online bundle for a purchase such as buy-one-get-one-free.
2. **Cross-marketing** – achieving the joint marketing efforts of both products through a distribution channel. Rather than the inclusion of the product within the packaging, instead offering a marketing opportunity to a partner brand within the distribution.

Online, offline and mobile all have their own distinct vaue in distribution of a partner brand in order to provide the most effective customer targeting. The more common forms include:

- In-store leaflets
- In-store coupons
- Magazine coupons
- In-store live demonstrations
- In-store TV demonstrations
- Email vouchers
- Mobile coupons
- QR codes

This is considered one of the most widespread types of brand partnerships, and one that has been practiced for decades. The reason for its popularity is due to the physical nature of the collaboration. It can physically place a partner brand in the hands of the target audience and visually places the partner brands alongside each other.

Both brands show a strong association and trust, and this resonates all the way to the customer, having a positive effect on loyalty and customer retention. Often the secondary brand will provide a primary brand an 'exclusive' offer or discount. This adds a huge advantage to the sales potential.

The act of distributing a partner's brand within your own store and alongside your own products is one of the purest and most recognisable types of brand partnership.

3. Sharing-Store-Space

"Where a partner provides an area of agreed space within their own store for the other partner's brand. The primary brand has rented out, provided or extended their retail outlet to integrate the secondary brand, for additional value to their consumers."

Shared-store partnerships are a growing phenomenon with some of the biggest brand names teaming up, but this isn't just reserved for retail outlets, it too can be found online:

1. **Offline** – the most common type of shared-store partnership. Offline we refer to the physical world where petrol stations, retail outlets, supermarkets and coffee shops have all been found to merge stores.
2. **Online** – a relatively new concept but one that is increasing in popularity. Online it is where both brands look to be associated alongside another by combining areas of their websites together through iFraming or creating dedicated sections.

Shared-Store partnerships offline and online can be further broken down into various forms:

Offline:

1. **Store within a store** – the classic form of a shared-store partnership is to provide a section of the primary brand's retail space for another brand – as shown in the example below with Cineworld and Starbucks. This adds value to the consumer base by offering an additional proposition to their shopping experience.

2. **Permanent desk** – this is where a primary brand provides a permanent desk for a partner brand. Department stores such as Selfridges or John Lewis often provide areas such this in their cosmetics section.

3. **Promotional stand** – occasionally a store will offer some of their space as a promotional stand. This provides a partner brand with an exclusive area dedicated to their product often manned by the brand's own personnel.

Lego featuring within one of the largest U.K. toy stores, The Entertainer, with promotional stands

Online:

1. **Dedicated tab or page** – providing a specific tab or page for a partner brand within the primary brand's website. This provides a dedicated area for added-value.

2. **Members area** – a members area provides exclusive material or content, this is therefore a popular area for partner brands to be featured.
3. **iFraming / Widget** – displaying a partners webpage via an iframe or widget within your own website. iFraming acts as a window that shows a relevant section of their site.

What's hugely beneficial about this strategy, particularly offline, is that it places the partner brand physically in front of consumers within a store. It's the ideal way to interact, touch and test a partner brand product. By being alongside one another this creates a powerful perception and by sharing retail space it minimises overall costs, attracts new consumers, and retains existing ones for longer.

Saying this, it is not without its risks; for a primary brand it will have to sacrifice a portion of its store for another that they may find doesn't resonate as strongly as they hoped. This may have negative connotations and in instances actually deter customers.

4. Joint Content

"Content Marketing is the creation of relevant content that will be highly engaging to customers. Content partnerships are the development of such content in collaboration with a partner brand that is then shared or promoted to respective target audiences."

There are two main ways a brand can partake in content partnerships:

1. **Co-creation** – both brands collaborate to create the content. This could be industry trends, market research, product releases or thought-leadership papers. By writing the content together and referencing one another's products it will align both brands for mutual recognition.
2. **Link sharing** – the primary brand creates the content but works in partnership with a secondary to promote it. Link sharing means linking to the partner's content from their

own site. This provides exposure, aligns both brands together, and advances SEO.

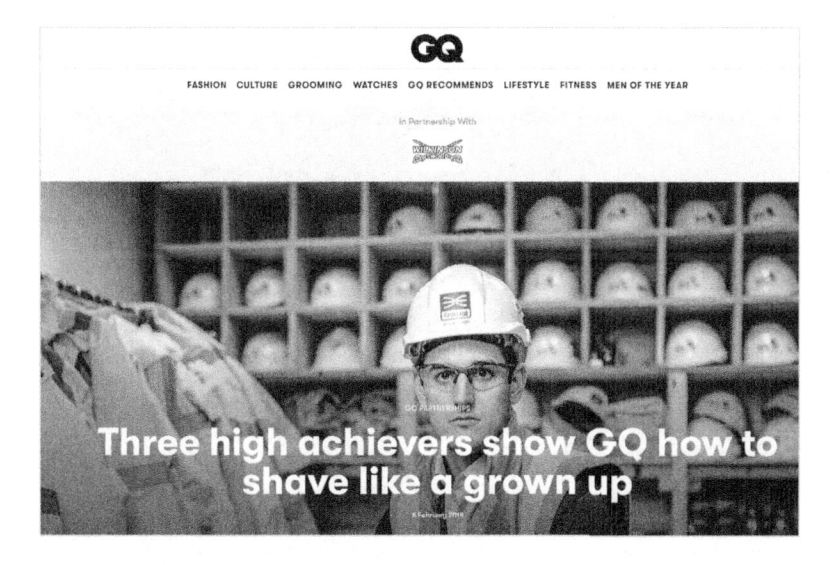

GQ and Wilkinson Sword combine with a joint content about shaving targeted GQ's male-centric audience.

Content partnerships can take various different formats, such as:

- **White papers** – presenting the latest industry research, advice, knowledge and trends using thought-leadership.

- **Articles** – featuring the latest joint products, opinions or promotions. These can take the form of reviews, how-to guides or case-studies.
- **Infographics** – a visual representation of information or data. Extremely effective for the use of joint brand imagery amongst the content.
- **Videos & podcasts** – the joint creation of a video or spoken media. Utilising the likes of YouTube to engage with the target audience.

SEO is now such an important aspect of digital marketing that specialist agencies have arisen, dedicated jobs created, and millions spent. Success in search rankings can literally make or break a business, making it the 21st century's most talked about marketing topic.

The evolution of websites has now reached the point where each page should ultimately evoke an action to convert viewers into paying customers. This means the greater numbers to a site the better chance of conversions and therefore revenues. This is the reason millions are spent climbing the ladder of Google's rankings.

Organic traffic via search engine optimisation is governed by a complex well-guarded algorithm made up of a huge number of variables, such as keyword usage, trusted inbound links and subject relevance. This means that your 'content is king' – how it is constructed, who likes it and how it is shared has direct influence on traffic, therefore conversions and ultimately sales.

SEO is not the only means to achieving traffic; social media has a huge part to play too. Channels such as Facebook and Twitter can guide vast quantities of traffic to your site depending on what you have to say and your shared content.

To ensure traffic remains high from both SEO and social the information that consumers receive must be fresh, relevant, and engaging. It also has to answer their questions, fulfil their needs and attract their attention. So this is where content partnerships comes in.

The fact is, one brand can create appealing content, but by providing fresh material in conjunction with a partner suddenly makes it an entirely new proposition, one that is far more interesting, likeable and engaging. This will attract the attention of both customer bases and affiliated parties. All this means a much larger network that will interact and share it. From an SEO and social engagement perspective the benefits are vast.

Let's consider, too, the cost effectiveness of such a partnership; utilising each other's personnel, resources and industry knowledge to produce the content is of huge value to both. While the utilisation of one another's digital channels and expertise will mean a lower end cost per acquired customer per content piece produced.

5. Joint Products & Integrations

"When two brands agree to create a new product or alter an existing product in order to provide additional value to the customer. Often the product is an amalgamation of both products aimed at mutual target audiences."

For brands partaking in joint product partnerships there are many factors to consider. Bearing in mind the huge impact on internal product departments, they are presented with three main collaboration choices:

1. **Powered by** – a partner brand supplying their services to benefit a new or existing product. Often software providers will provide their technologies for a product. Mobile phones powered by a technology provider such as Google or Microsoft is a good example.
2. **White label** – many successful technologies also offer white label solutions. This means selling off their services or leasing their technology for a partner brand. The partner brand then utilises it under its own brand name.

3. **Product merger** – a merger is where both brands have decided to amalgamate their products together. This too comes in various formats, from full to partial mergers depending on the product line.

These alliances can be very interesting for an organisation's product portfolio, the result is a fresh line of innovative product solutions. With the breakthrough of digital technologies over the past decade we are now seeing a far greater increase in such partnerships. There are four specific forms that have emerged:

1. **New Product Launch** – two firms may decide to launch a brand new product, one that amalgamates both brands under an exciting new concept. Both companies leverage each other's brand image, reputation, resources, and market reach – as shown in the example below with Apple and Nike who combined to create the 'The Nike & iPod Sports Kit'.

2. **Brand leveraging** – rather than a full product merger often just the branding is joined. With such product partnerships it is about utilising the partners design and packaging.

3. **New markets** – by partnering products together a popular firm in the US seeking new customers from Europe might collaborate with a successful European brand to enter this new market, and with this the joint product might have to adapt to the new market.

4. **Sharing costs** – occasionally a product partnership will purely be a cost-saving exercise. This is achieved with the

sharing of resources and expertise; this in turn reduces cost of production and marketing.

The main consideration with this kind of partnership is that they are a product and marketing initiative involving the buy-in from both departments. Any alterations to a product would have to be planned for; sales departments briefed on alterations, with marketing prepared for go-to-market campaigns.

An effective go-to-market strategy will require a distinct value proposition. The unique selling point of the joint product must be communicated to highlight these new product features and their benefits to a consumer. Branding is also important, getting this right will ensure that the primary brand's look and feel is displayed not only through the packaging but also via all advertising channels effectively.

It is fair to say that this is probably the most innovative type of Brand Partnership but one that does not come without its complications. If the product misses the mark and the value proposition fails to resonate with the target audience it would certainly be deemed a very expensive failure.

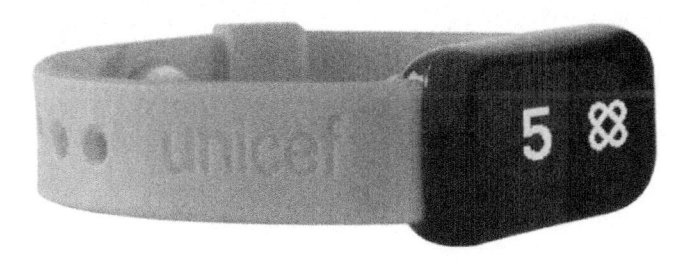

Joint Product integration with Unicef and Fitbit

The future of brand interactions looks like Creme Egg mayonnaise

Heinz and Cadbury's Creme Egg integrating their products

6. Product Placements

"The subtle placement of a brand within a media channel. It is deemed a cross-over of sponsorship and advertising that works well in-partnership with high grossing TV and Film productions and brands within their own right. E.g. Star Wars"

Product placement partnerships comes in three main types. These reflect the ways in which products are placed within the media, a decision made through the coalition of brand and media channel:

1. **Subtle placement** – where the inclusion of the brand logo, a background shot of the product, or an elusive hint towards a products usage, is found within TV and film scenes.
2. **Direct advertising** – aside from subtle placement there is a more direct approach. More obvious placement advertising within a media programme, such as a cookery show endorsing a product, is deemed direct.
3. **Public person sponsorship** – there can be a fine line between product placement and sponsorship. Away from TV and film there is also the placement through the use of celebrity endorsements who are encouraged to wear the clothing or use a product. When a brand sends a celebrity free items they are seeking product placement, often

through paparazzi photos, social media and usage in their daily lives.

Once a brand has established a relationship with an agency acting on their behalf or in collaboration directly with a TV studio or film production company, placement can take the following forms:

- Logo within frame or scene
- Direct mention or usage
- Inclusion in plot
- Background placement
- Visible foreground placement
- Celebrity endorsement

Even though it is currently one of the least used types of Brand Partnership let's not take away its extremely innovative attributes. Although often subtle there are a number of smart ways in which to achieve exposure.

When it comes to such niche forms of marketing as this there are always brands that perfect it better than others. Larger brands in particular find they can leverage its qualities more so than smaller ones. Often the reason comes down to the network, celebrity, or media in question, they only wish to work with such brands that will resonate with the audience; the Apple's, Facebook's and Pepsi's of this world.

Although, saying this, smaller brands running product placement via celebrity endorsements (Influencers) often notice soars in sales and overnight recognition; a fashion brand that places their products in the hands of a well-known public figure, that is advertised on Instagram, is likely to see their popularity surge.

7. Licensing Schemes

"Licensing is a business arrangement in which one company gives another company permission to manufacture its product using its brand image for an agreed payment."

There are two ways that a brand will choose to collaborate with another when it comes to licensing partnership:

1. **Sold** – most brands that decide to license their brand choose to sell it to their partners for a given price. This provides them access to various assets (described below) to improve their product or service offering.
2. **Collaborative** – some brands decide to get involved in the licensing partnership and actively collaborate with the partner. This has close associations with joint product partnerships where a company may utilise another's product and brand image to provide an exclusive unique offering.

There are many ways a company who licenses another's brand can utilise it. After purchasing the right to use their brand they can work on the following:

- **Logo** – the logo of another brand can be used within a company's own product line to enhance it.
- **Brand image** – the brand image itself can comprise not only the logo but the colours, font and tone of voice.
- **Reputation** – with the purchase of any brand comes with it its reputation; utilising this to a company's advantage in their new product offering.
- **Culture** – with a brand's reputation also comes its company culture. A company can utilise the ethics and company values this also brings.
- **Design** – the design assets that come with a brand can also be utilised within the firm's products or services.

The creation of a brand, one with a stand-out reputation, is extremely time consuming and costly. So for many organisations the quickest and simplest way is to purchase it. This is what licensing offers a company; tying in a global brand to the product hugely enhances it.

A product can go from mediocre to a sales success very swiftly if the right brand is licensed and leveraged accordingly. Simply using the brands name for the product and attaching the logo to it, even if the product hasn't changed at all from previous editions, can lead to a huge surge in sales. This is a type of partnership that some may say is a sales technique rather than marketing, but it involves the use of branding which can affect the entire marketing proposition and how it is positioned.

8. Loyalty & Discounts

"A retention marketing technique that offers consumers a reward in return for increased usage. A loyalty partnership enhances the typical model by offering consumers partner

offers to encourage longevity and increased purchase frequency."

Loyalty partnership marketing comes in three specific types. All of which relate to how consumers are loyal to a brand:

1. **Frequency** – loyalty can be rewarded based on frequency of customer use; the more a product is bought or a service used the more rewards a consumer receives. A reward can be a partner brand discount; smart brands take this a step further by personalising, providing an offer in conjunction with a partner brand tailored to the consumer based on their spending patterns or personal profile.
2. **Volume** – the alternative is to reward based on amount purchased; where the higher the number bought the larger the reward. Savvy brands provide varying degrees of reward to those that purchase larger amounts, often fully personalising the offer.

3. **Advocate** – the third type is often described as advocacy; where a consumer is so loyal to a brand they will support it and promote it, with this a brand will offer extended rewards. It is a type of loyalty that focuses purely on rewarding those who shout about a brand and even have the power to influence others.

A brand can encourage consumer loyalty in a number of ways. The following examples can be adjusted depending on consumer base segments:

- Loyalty club/scheme
- Loyalty cards/vouchers
- One-off rewards
- Free money, gifts, raffles
- Seasonal promotions
- Product extensions

All of these offer the possibility for partner brand involvement, mainly by including their discounts or exclusive products within the loyalty program. As a technique it allows two brands to successfully align their proposition with each other utilising their similar databases to improve customer retention rates.

This is a type of Brand Partnership that has been tried and tested by a number of high profile brand names, which highlights it as one of the most effective types. A loyal collaboration can enhance the image of a brand, acquire a vast number of new customers who already contain the proven characteristics of being loyal, and increases the spend frequency and volume growth.

CommuterClub featuring brand offers on their website to benefit their customers.

9. Non-profit and Charitable

"A primary brand sponsors or markets itself with a charitable organisation or cause. In turn they seek exposure, promotion, or donations"

Benefits can be very fruitful when working with a charitable cause. We have pin-pointed two main reasons why a primary brand would do partner with a charity:

1. **Cultural influence** – a brand can primarily work with a charitable brand to offer a moral contribution. This is part of company culture and often attributable to the attitudes of senior stakeholders.
2. **Brand leverage** – some firms prefer to associate themselves due to the benefits it brings to their consumer and public reputation.

Charitable partnerships can take a number of forms, with various ways in which a brand and charity can run such campaigns. These include exhibitions, public events, award shows, sponsorship, raffle contributions and news stories.

As today's customer is more industry aware and savvy with their purchasing decisions, with abundant comparison and review sites at their fingertips, a brand that upholds a strong public reputation is increasingly standing out from the crowd. Associating your brand to a charitable cause is therefore fast becoming the main method to securing such a status.

Innocent Smoothies for example, one of the most reputable drinks companies in the UK, stressing the importance of fair-trade production, also associate themselves with a number of charities via their Innocent Foundation. Firms such as this that can leverage a Charitable Partnership for marketing purposes will see their public reputation and brand image vastly enhanced.

10. Sponsorships

"The marketing tactic of placing a brand alongside a particular event, displaying itself as a partner or supporter, with the objective to increase brand recognition and reputation."

Sponsorship has been around since the dawn of marketing and one of the most successful ways to create a brand identity. There are various objectives to sponsorship and these lie under three key banners:

1. **Awareness** – aligning a product alongside an event for mass exposure is the most common type of Sponsorship. The aim is to have the largest possible reach of your brand to both existing and new consumers.

2. **Association** – linking the product with a cause, person, or event to provide a brand association in the eyes of the consumer. Every time you think of that event you will tie that in with the sponsored brand too.

3. **Consumer understanding** – sponsorship can link a brand proposition with an event so that it provides product education to the consumer. Some propositions are more complex than others so sponsorship is seen as an effective way to teach a consumer what the product can offer.

Sponsorship comes in many shapes and sizes. Below are several varieties that are commonly found across many of the world's popular partnerships:

- **Sporting sponsorships** – some of the most expensive yet effective forms of brand exposure. They can be found within every popular sport from team sponsorships, stadium names, board advertisements, and player endorsements.
- **Media sponsorship** – any sponsorship found within TV, film and radio are all forms of media sponsorships; the sponsoring of a new television series is a great example. It is an effective tactic for mass brand awareness.
- **Event sponsorship** – the World Cup, Olympics, and charity events such as the London Marathon, are all examples of this. The Olympics was in such high demand for London 2012 that there were sponsors for nearly every possible association: drinks, supermarkets, and even an official furniture sponsor.
- **Local sponsorship** – a niche but highly effective form where local businesses look for exposure towards a specific market. Local farmers market, charity events and political

conventions, all provide a brand the opportunity for exposure.

- **Seal of approval** – with foods, health products and luxury items such as holidays a seal of approval is a powerful tool. When a hotel or restaurant has the TripAdvisor certificate displayed it provides that seal of approval we know and trust.

For decades global brands such as Coca Cola, McDonald's, Pepsi, O2, Nokia, Red Bull and British Airways all pour billions of marketing spend into sponsorships, and the reasons are plentiful. They increases brand reach, increase brand awareness, improves brand trust, change a brand's value proposition or image, improve product understanding and open up new global or local markets.

The benefits are a clear justification for companies acting on sponsorship marketing, but for some marketers they like to stay clear due to several distinct drawbacks:

- **Difficult to track performance** – other than the media value earned, noticing the increase in overall sales from a sponsorship campaign can be difficult. There is very little to tag a campaign and go by as often it is simply just a branded logo that's displayed. The fact is the performance will never be as accurate tracked as some forms of digital marketing.
- **Difficult to quantify** – can the costs be quantified accurately in comparison to the media value earned? Numbers can become vague in sponsorship; many feel the true value of new acquisition cannot confidently be associated with the sponsorship.
- **How to trigger sales and conversion?** – At the end of the day brands must focus on conversion, but sponsorship offers no clear call to action. Brand recognition that isn't purely quantifiable is the main advantage rather than direct sales.

Despite this, sponsorship has been tried and tested by the most well know global brands out there, therefore it is, aside from the caveats, trusted and relied upon, making it a vital Brand Partnership technique.

The Commerzbank Arena in Frankfurt, Germany - major brands are now sponsoring items as large as stadiums and clubs are adopting brand names for stadium names.

Chapter 3: There are actually only 3 core types

There are many guides asking the big question; what are brand partnerships? Many describe the 10 types mentioned above, but we can take this a step further...

If you think about it the 10 types can be broken down further into 3 core types;

1. **Integrations**
2. **Reward**
3. **Awareness**

As we go through each of the 3 core types, you will see how each of the 10 types fit into one of these categories...

- *Loyalty, Affiliation* and *Content* are all types of **Reward Partnership**.
- *Distribution, Licencing, Shared Stores* and *Joint Products* can all be described as **Integration Partnerships**.
- *Sponsorship, Product Placement*, and *Charitable* partnerships are all versions of **Awareness Partnerships,** where one brand aims to improve its brand recognition.

1. Integration Partnerships

What are Integration Partnerships?

An Integrated Partnership takes all the elements of the traditional partnership model but taking it a step further where a primary brand will include the secondary's product into their own.

What is the aim of an Integration Partnership?

The aim of integrating another product into your own is to provide additional value to the customer. Above all, you're taking the benefits of their product and adding it to your own. You're including their USP to complement what you already offer.

Genius & Spotify — Integration Partnership - Spotify integrated Genius into it's app to provide instant lyrics.

What are the main types of Integration Partnership?

1. Joint Products
2. iFraming or Widgets
3. API Integrations
4. White labels

Why run Integration Partnerships?

- Promote a product that you don't already offer

- Monetisation or commission
- Brand Leveraging
- As a reward or discount
- To upsell your products
- To attract their customers ahead of competitors

2. Reward Partnerships

What are Reward Partnerships?

Reward Partnerships are where one brand provides a discounted offer to their service for the other brand to promote. For the primary brand they benefit from new customer acquisition, for the secondary they achieve revenue via commissions.

What is the aim of a Reward Partnership?

Reward Partnerships are one of the purest forms of partnerships. Taking another brand and promoting it on your site was taken from the affiliate/advertising model, but now has far closer links to partnerships — where primary brands offer special places for brand rewards such as discount pages. While secondary brands look to offer exclusive offers to acquire their customers.

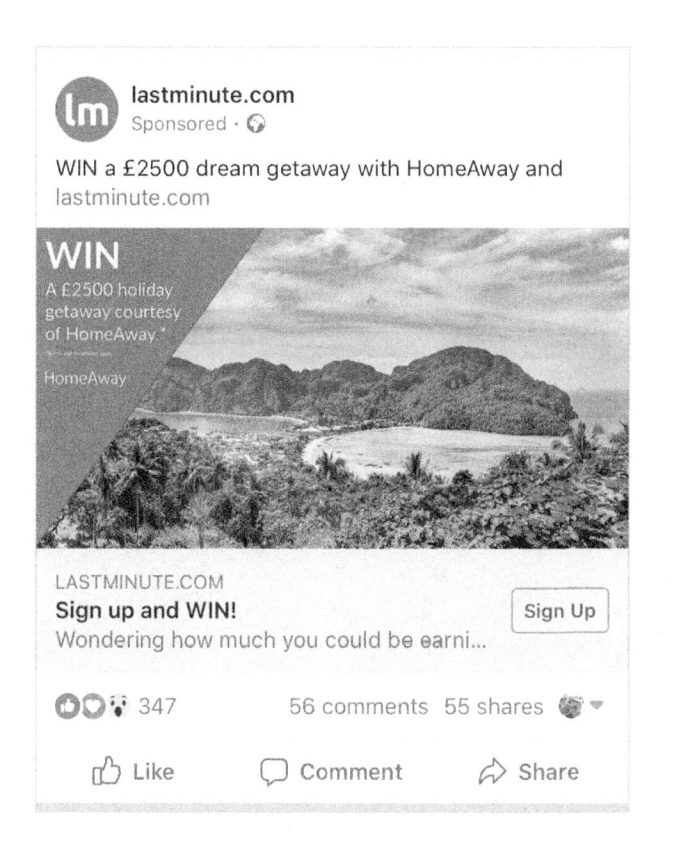

What are the main types of Reward Partnership?

1. Discount
2. Additional Value
3. Promotions
4. Loyalty Schemes

Why run Reward Partnerships?

- Upsell
- Earn commission
- Additional value to customers
- Loyalty to increase customer LTV
- Brand Association

3. Awareness Partnerships

What are Awareness Partnerships?

Awareness Partnerships involve one brand promoting another for the primary brand to achieve brand recognition. Brands partaking in these types of partnerships are essentially involved in sponsorships, joint events and product placements.

What is the aim of an Awareness Partnership?

These partnerships are for brands aiming to raise brand awareness via association with the right partner brand. Many of us are familiar with these techniques, whether it be partnering with a brand at a joint event, using an influencer or sponsoring a charity.

Emirates sponsoring the Arsenal FC stadium

What are the main types of Awareness Partnership?

- Sponsorships
- Product Placements
- Influencers
- Events

Why run Awareness Partnerships?

- Brand awareness
- Brand association
- Charitable causes
- Improved brand perception

Remember there are cross-overs between types

Can a Charitable partnership also be a Reward partnership? Can content also be considered an Awareness partnership?

It's important to mention, partnership types are always fluid. In other words, there is huge cross-over between types. There is not always one fixed model to describe a particular type. Partnerships can be as unique as the brands involved and can be more than one at any one time.

Chapter 4: Examples of Brand Partnerships

Brand Partnerships, Partnership Marketing or Co-marketing — whichever you choose to call it, is proving to be one of the most popular emerging marketing methods over the last few years to achieve long-term growth. We have seen the emergence of some of the world's best known brands exploring this space. Here are some examples:

Exclusive offering from E.ON and Tesco

E.ON is one Europe's largest energy service providers. Based in Germany they operate in over 30 countries to over 33 million customers.

Tesco is a British multinational supermarket chain. It is the third-largest retailer in the world measured by profits and second-largest retailer in the world measured by revenues. It has stores across Europe and Asia.

The E.ON and Tesco partnership is an excellent example of a Loyalty campaign offering UK customers the exclusive option to exchange Tesco Clubcard vouchers to pay their E.ON energy bills.

Here a whole host of campaign elements were agreed upon, from featuring the offer in E.ON newsletters, exposure onsite and within direct mail, as well as the agreed communication strategy, tone of voice, use of Tesco branding, and decisions on customer segments and offer terms.

E.ON Rewards

Thanks for opting in to get E.ON Rewards Points. You'll be able to get your points when you switch to one of our electricity or Dual Fuel tariffs that offer them. There's no exit fee for switching, but the scheme's ending soon.

If you signed up on our older Tesco Clubcard points scheme (before 6 December 2013), you'll change to our current E.ON Rewards Points scheme as soon as you switch to one of our tariffs that offer them.

You'll be able to find out what tariffs offer Rewards by checking section 14 of your tariff's T&Cs.

You have **2600** E.ON Reward Points

1 E.ON Reward Point = 1 Tesco Clubcard point

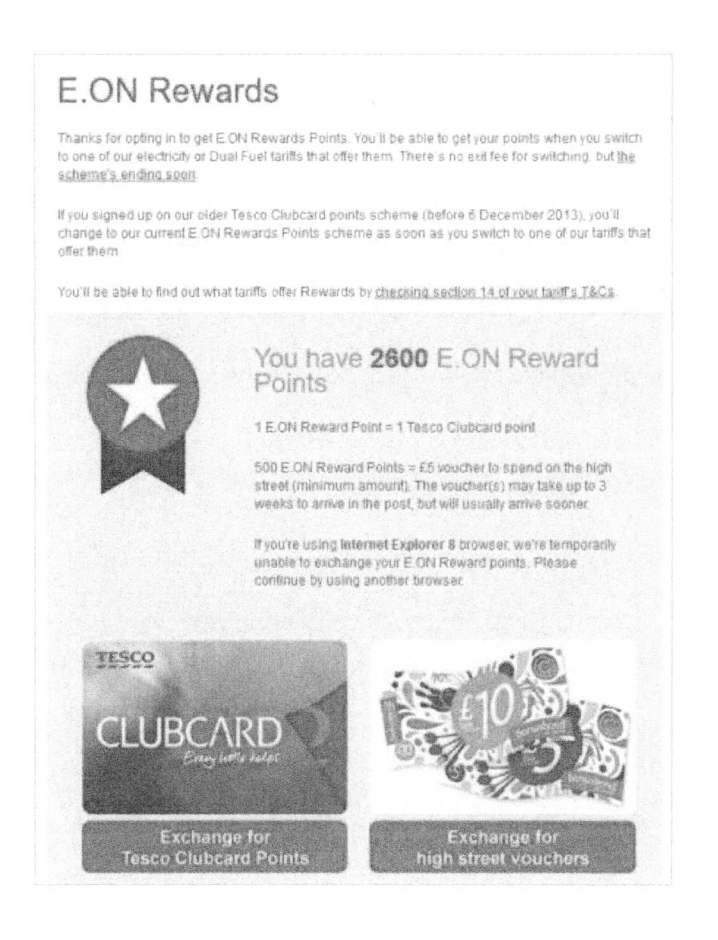

500 E.ON Reward Points = £5 voucher to spend on the high street (minimum amount). The voucher(s) may take up to 3 weeks to arrive in the post, but will usually arrive sooner.

If you're using **Internet Explorer 8** browser, we're temporarily unable to exchange your E.ON Reward points. Please continue by using another browser.

Exchange for Tesco Clubcard Points

Exchange for high street vouchers

Travel at a discount with Virgin Trains & Festival No6

Virgin Trains as a brand aim to portray efficiency and comfort while aiming to bring back the elegance of train travel.

Festival N°6 is an annual art and music festival held at Portmeirion, Wales. The festival presents a wide range of music genres including folk, house and dance. Their headliners include acts like Grace Jones and Belle & Sebastian.

Here Virgin Trains have partnered with the popular festival to become their exclusive travel partner, offering attendees advanced tickets at 25% discount.

This partnership promotes Virgin to all festival-goers as the transportation of choice to the difficult to reach location. By doing so they stand out ahead of their competitor operators. They also portray themselves as both trendy and highly innovative.

For Festival N°6 it provides expansive customer reach via Virgin's communication emails, competitions, and exclusive online PR content.

Marks & Spencer and BP share a store

In 2005 BP signed an agreement with Marks & Spencer to improve the overall service station experience and increase the purchase offering to consumers.

For BP it leverages the upper-class M&S Food brand image, adding value, setting them apart from competitor service stations. This is such a successful partnership that is now found in over 120 locations nationwide.

Metro highlight eHarmony in newsletter exposure

The Metro is the most popular free newspaper in the U.K. with over 2 million readers, mostly distributed for commuters on the transport network.

eHarmony is one of the strongest online dating brands to have emerged in the market, focusing on compatibility and exact matches.

eHarmony collaborated with Metro to provide a dedicated promotion where readers receive a special discount by using the provided PromoCode. Here Metro offered their newsletter as an asset.

They helped to sell in the partnership by highlighting the number of relevant consumers it would be visible to, and eHarmony reciprocated by creating the exclusive offering just for Metro users.

Consistent terminology

For the 10 types of brand partnerships, described above, and the 3 core types, it's important to also understand the terminology that goes alongside them. The subject currently suffers from a distinct lack of consistency when it comes to the terminology used. Upon billboards, online ads, and loyalty schemes, many of the terms detailed below have been used to illustrate a partnership between two brands. They are recognisable terms although ones that are not always entirely accurate.

Here are a few definitions:

- ***In partnership with*** – the most popular phrase used to describe a partnership with another brand, literally says what it means; informing consumers that there is a collaboration occurring and that the partnership will benefit both primary and secondary brands as well as ultimately the consumer.
- ***Supported by*** – commonly found within charitable partnerships. Being supported by a partner brand refers to one brand assisting the other in the campaign. It portrays an element of comfort towards a consumer, showing the cause is backed by a reputable brand.

- ***Certified by*** – provides authenticity to the partnership. By stating that a brand certifies another delivers trust to the consumer that the offering is backed by the supporting brand.
- ***Incorporating*** – generally means '*together with*' and relates to a primary brand including a secondary brands proposition within their own. If a major brand is incorporating with another it is referencing the fact that they are providing their services as an add-on or an extra.
- ***Powered by*** – often refers to the presence of a partner brand supplying their services to benefit another product. An example of this is the Nexus phone which is '*Powered by*' Google. Such a partnership ultimately benefits the consumer with a far superior product utilising both technologies.
- ***In association with*** – most commonly used when both brands have an equal role to play in the partnership. The term association means that both brands have agreed on a mutual partnership offering.

Chapter 5: What's the difference between Affiliate Marketing and Brand Partnerships?

Affiliate marketing is one of the 10 types of Brand Partnerships, but there is often confusion between the two, and what actually makes it one of the partnership types, even though it's also a stand-alone marketing channel in its own right - a bit like Sponsorship. Let's now discuss the fundamental differences between them.

What is Affiliate Marketing?

Good-old Wikipedia Definition:

Affiliate marketing is a type of performance-based marketing in which a business rewards one or more affiliates for each visitor or customer brought by the affiliate's own marketing efforts.

Refined Definition:

Affiliate Marketing is a performance marketing technique where websites, otherwise known as publishers, will promote your product or service in return for a monetary reward.

What are the fundamental differences?

1. Affiliate marketing focuses on CPA (cost per acquisition) and an advertiser to publisher relationship, while Partnerships should always try to be reciprocal and mutual – to elaborate on this, affiliate marketing often involves an advertiser paying a publisher for every referred customer and sale they send to them. This is known as a CPA, and although other commission methods are possible, this essentially describes the relationship between advertiser and publisher. The advertiser is looking for customers from the publisher's user/reader base.

A partnership on the other hand should always try to be more than that. It focuses on not just a one-way distinction, but a mutual relationship where both can benefit. As described previously, Affiliate marketing can also be a type of partnership marketing because at the end of the day there is a benefit for both, except that for the advertiser it's often monetary.

The main purpose of partnerships though is to take affiliate marketing a step further than monetary, and to provide more than simply a tracking link and the passing of CPA.

2. Partnerships are often brand to brand, while affiliate marketing is content site to brand site relationship – this continues on the above point, as affiliate marketing focuses on an advertiser to publisher relationship, while partnerships are both advertiser-advertiser, as well as advertiser-publisher.

The advertiser is normally a brand that sells something or provides a service. While the publisher tends to be one that publishers an advert, often in a form of content, comparison table or cashback placing. Partnerships on the other hand tend to focus on a brand to brand relationships. This could in some ways be described as an advertiser to advertiser relationship.

Partnerships involve like-minded brands promoting each other to their databases. It's therefore a mutual relationship, where funds aren't always necessary to exchange between both parties. It can be a free promotion if the other brand is offering equal exposure in return.

3. Partnerships include integrations and more specialist scenarios like using products. While affiliation focuses on passing customers from one site to the next. Affiliation is about passing customers from one user/reader base, often one with tens of thousands of users such as a comparison site, to an advertiser brand to purchase their products.

While Partnerships are more specialist — it's more about integrating a brand's product within your own to truly benefit the customer — to provide ease or convenience to them.

An example of this is a bank that doesn't offer insurance products, nor has the capacity or experience to build an insurance offering, but they know there's an appetite from their customers for one. So, they reach out and partner with a like-minded insurance company and either white label their product or keep the branding and expose it to their base. As you can see this type of partnership takes affiliation a step further than just a monetary relationship or affiliate link.

Comparing the benefits of each

Whether one type of marketing is right over the other is completely dependant on the company, its objectives and experience in each area. Brand Partnerships might benefit one brand, while Affiliate Marketing may not.

There is a strong argument though that Brand Partnerships include so many elements of Affiliate Marketing, that it essentially encompasses it. Others say they are very distinct and both can be run by a company with positive effects.

Affiliate Marketing can bring an abundance of customers, some brands reporting 20% of their overall sales coming from this channel alone. Sites like cashback and comparison tables attract customers who are very much in-market. Publishers such as *Moneysavingexpert* claim to have 15 million subscribers to their newsletter – even at a click-through rate of 1% and a conversion rate of 1% that's 1,500 customers in one hit for an advertiser. The opposing view though is that these customers are often lower value than those from other channels. Reason being, cashback sites like Topcashback and Quidco, attract customers looking for deals. Deal-hunters, can be a big problem and give the affiliate industry a bad name. This is why some retail brands opt to not work with certain affiliate sites as they do not want to incentivise such behaviour and would rather the loyalty of customers coming from more other channels.

While Partnerships work with like-minded brands who have similar target audiences. So the audiences might not necessarily be in-market, which is a downside to partnership marketing, but they are more likely to be relevant customers and therefore loyal ones. They also give you that reach that might have otherwise been untapped. Partnerships also allow you to provide products and services you may not have had otherwise, therefore expanding your offering, reach, brand and your revenue.

In conclusion, it's a grey area. We've highlighted the debate above, showing how different they are but also included them as one of the 10 types of Brand Partnerships. So as you can see, it's not distinct or clear. Overall though both types are meant to achieve your goals via 'partnership' methods. And the benefits are dependant on what you want to achieve.

Chapter 6: How to decide which partners to work with

The 5 considerations to deciding your partners

Deciding which partners to work with comes with many considerations. Not all partners will be suitable to promote your brand. This is why the first consideration, before even going out to attract partners, is to know which brands would be the right fit for you.

1. You need to know your own brand

Firstly, how can you know if a partner is the right one to work with if you don't truly understand and know your own brand?

By that we mean, do you know what your brand stands for? Do you know your core product proposition? And do you know who your customers are?

These are vital questions to have a clear understanding of so that you can work with partners that resonate with your brand. Deciding which partners to work with, really does start with knowing who you are as a brand.

2. Having brand recognition

This brings us on to brand recognition and resonation. When it comes to partnerships, where both brands mutually promote each other, you want to work with brands that are both recognisable, as well as resonate with your audience.

A recognisable brand doesn't necessarily mean a big brand name, as long as it's recognisable with your audience. By resonation we mean, will your audience understand their proposition easily and vice versa?

Fundamentally other websites want to promote the most recognisable brands and the ones that they think their users are more likely to click through to and engage with. I.e. the ones with the highest conversion rates.

3. There should be 'Target Audience Similarity'

Another hugely important consideration is 'Target Audience Similarity'. For partnerships, it's logical that a brand you want to promote will be one with as large and as relevant an audience as possible. As well as one containing customers of a similar profile to your own.

As a Brand Partnership example, a brand that offers a savings app for millennials to get on the housing ladder will have a matching audience to a brand that offers a simplified online and in-app mortgage service tailored to first-time buyers. And the two apps would look at a syncing their products, either via a joint campaign or in-app integration.

4. Ensuring objective alignment

Any brand that has a similar objective to your own is definitely one to work with. By objective, we can mean two things.

- Either their general business proposition, i.e. what is their purpose or reason they exist?
- Or their marketing objective such as attracting new customers or increasing life-time value (LTV).

If brands have similar goals and a similar company purpose, then they're more likely to work together and far more likely to be the perfect fit.

Try to understand what the partner wants out of the partnership. What are their goals, expectations and forecasts? Consider all of these and see whether they fit with your own. They don't have to be the same, they don't have to be both acquisitions or earning commissions, but it's about creating a campaign that will suit both parties.

5. There's also location, growth and size to consider

Together with the above are the slightly less important but still relevant considerations...

- What about the location of a partner? For small business partnerships, often locality will be a deciding factor.
- How about company history and growth patterns? Brands with a similar history of growth can often see common ground.

- Company size can also be a factor, this is similar to brand recognition. Brands like to work with others of a similar size and structure.
- And lastly, having similar processes, sign-off procedures and schedules, will also make it a whole lot easier.

The importance of 'Partner-Friendly' Brands

To wrap this up, we like to use a collective term we call *Partner-Friendly Brands*. These are brands that tick the two most important areas of 1) *Brand Resonation* and 2) *Target Audience Similarity*. Brands should seek partners that match these two fundamental areas and can offer an audience that will grow the other's business.

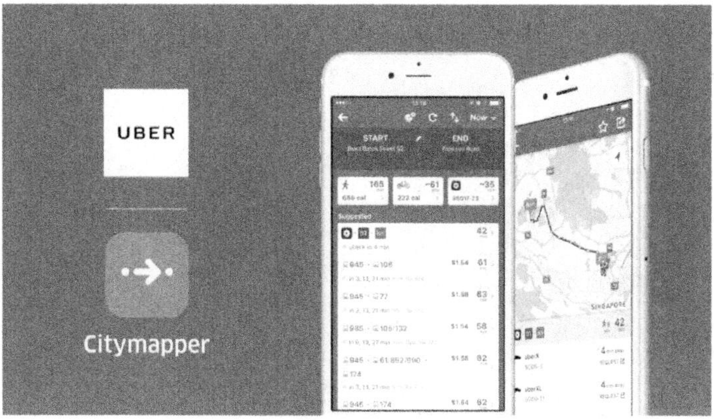
UBER
Citymapper

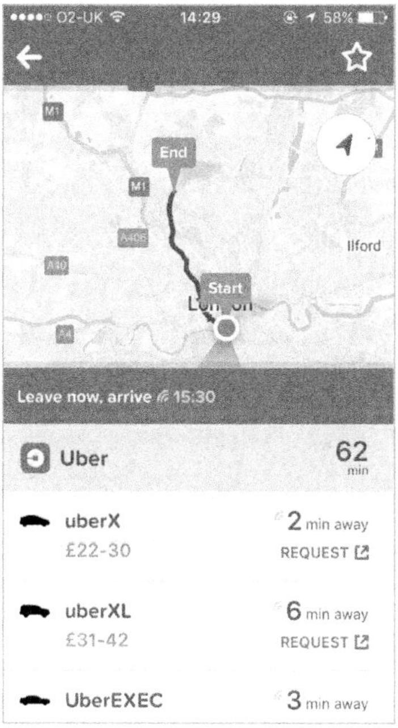
O2-UK
14:29
58%
M1
End
M1
A406
A40
Ilford
Start
London
A4
Leave now, arrive 15:30
Uber
62
min
uberX
£22-30
2 min away
REQUEST
uberXL
£31-42
6 min away
REQUEST
UberEXEC
3 min away

Example of 'Partner-Friendly Brands' — Uber & Citymapper complement each other with their 'target audience similarity'.

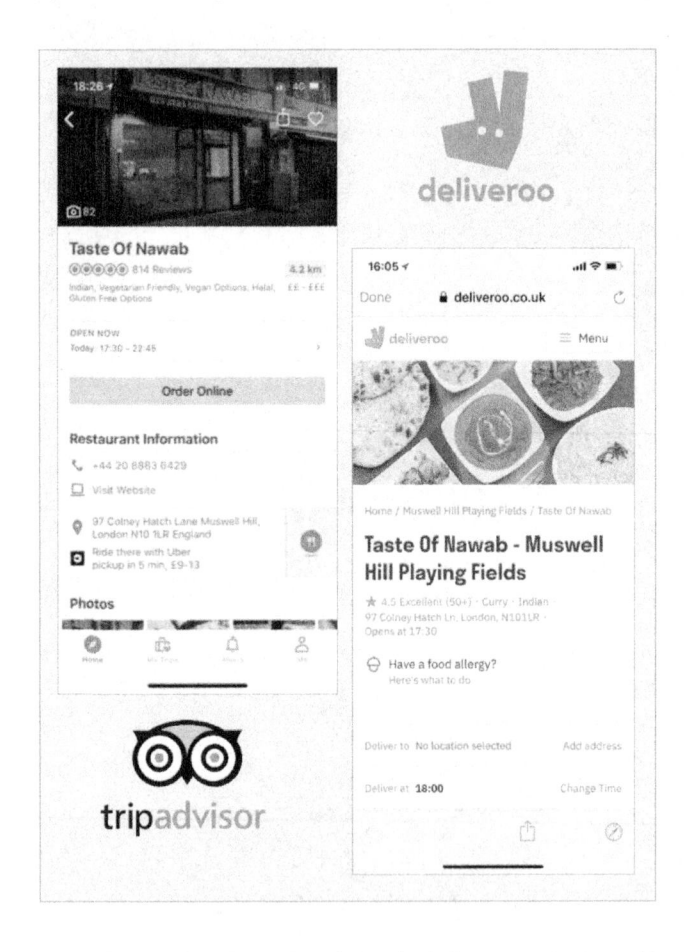

Deliveroo and TripAdvisor are Partner-Friendly brands who have teamed up to provide instant ordering of a restaurant in the TripAdvisor platform.

The key is often audience size and engagement

If a brand has a large enough audience who are receptive to third party offers, then they are one to work with. Size is often such an important factor because often with the uptake of your products via third-party sites, you need enough traffic volume flowing through for there to be decent conversion rates. Take MoneySavingExpert's newsletter for example, this has 15+ million recipients, which means each partner represented on there will each attract several hundred thousand click through's.

We should note with the above, it's not necessarily about volume. It's more about volume quality. Because you want the right customers clicking through, rather than hundreds of thousands of wasted leads. So often a partner with 10k quality customers who will convert at a higher rate or of higher basket size, are far more valuable than 1m customers who convert at a far lower percentage.

Secondly, if you can offer a product that fulfils a desire or need from that third party audience, or as mentioned, you can supply an attractive offer or discount that they'll uptake, then a partnership will be a success. Look for partners that are receptive to third party offers. Perhaps they have an offers area, or loyalty club, where your brand will fit in nicely.

Many brands have such an area now, Santander have a link from the users dashboard to an offers area, Tesco have their Clubcard, PayPal have a special discounts section, and British Gas have their rewards. Exclusive offers are perfect for high engagement and certainly one to utilise with the right partners. See this example below...

The Guardian and Audible Offer Listeners Exclusive Content

Founded in 1821, Guardian News & Media publishes guardian.co.uk, guardiannews.com and the Guardian and Observer newspapers. The newspaper's combined print and online editions reach nearly 9 million readers.

Audible Inc. is an Amazon company, a leading provider of digital spoken audio entertainment. Audible's content includes more than 100,000 programs from more than 1,800 providers that include leading audiobook publishers, broadcasters, entertainers, magazines and newspaper providers.

The Guardian and Audible partnered together to form The Guardian Audio Edition, an hour-long weekly audio digest. Each edition aimed to showcase the very best news, culture and opinion pieces published in the Guardian that week. The Guardian Audio Edition forms part of a wider partnership between the Guardian and Audible that includes sponsorship of the Guardian books homepage, their weekly podcast and their book review pages.

All activity is supported by co-branded advertising across the Guardian, including digital ads on their site and print ads in their main paper. In conclusion, this partnership is a great example of utilising exclusivity to offer consumers something that truly adds value.

Consider competitors and partner mix

Also, look at your competitors. If they are working with a third party, then can you displace them?

It's also a telling sign that that type of partnership works. So if you can't displace them, why not approach similar third party sites to those and set up a replica partnership arrangement.

Another important factor to review is whether a partner will contribute to your existing channel mix. In affiliate marketing, you can often segment your types of third party sites into; content, cashback, voucher, freebie, loyalty etc. Therefore if you locate a partner site and wish to determine whether to work with it or not, then ask yourself does it fit into my current mix?

If you already have plenty of content affiliates, will another overcrowd that one segment so that you are now overlying on it. You never want to weigh your affiliate mix too heavily on one affiliate type.

The same applies for size of affiliates within your mix. Will your new publisher site contribute to this mix? Is it worth adding another long-tail? Or will another super-affiliate help balance the reliance on other large partners?

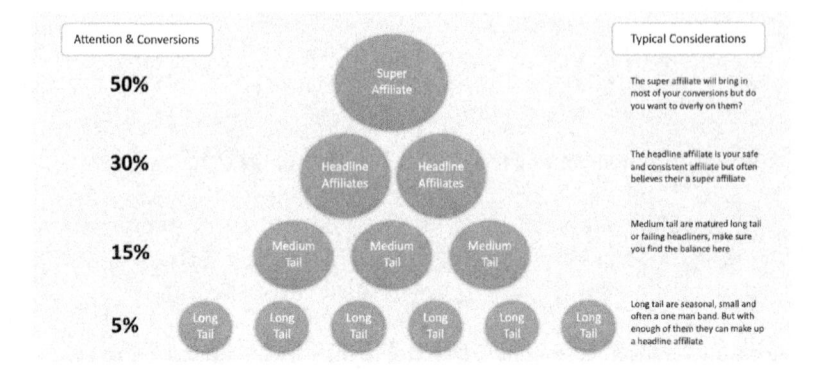

Attention & Conversions		Typical Considerations
50%	Super Affiliate	The super affiliate will bring in most of your conversions but do you want to overly on them?
30%	Headline Affiliates / Headline Affiliates	The headline affiliate is your safe and consistent affiliate but often believes their a super affiliate
15%	Medium Tail / Medium Tail / Medium Tail	Medium tail are matured long tail or failing headliners, make sure you find the balance here
5%	Long Tail × 6	Long tail are seasonal, small and often a one man band. But with enough of them they can make up a headline affiliate

This shows a typical affiliate channel mix, with super to long-tail affiliates. It's all about finding a balance, so judge whether this new partner you're considering will actually help balance your existing mix. While of course, contributing to growth and bringing in new customers.

The importance of forging strong relationships

When it comes to recruiting new partners, the reputation from your existing partners says a lot. Not only do testimonials and recommendations work wonderfully, but the connections existing partners also have is extremely powerful – after all, word spreads – so it goes without saying, treat your existing partners well and others will come flocking.

Imagine a scenario where you take a small one-man website partner out on a VIP occasion, they enjoy themselves, value the advice you gave them over a beer or two, and highly appreciated your hospitality. Back at the desk, you answer their emails within 24 hours, you respond politely answering all their needs – you even go as far as making friends with them. Well, this reputation will spread. The one-man partner will know others, and soon he has referred 3 or 4 more brand partners to you.

Take this a step further and he introduces you to a former colleague at one of the largest brands, who via his recommendation, is keen to work with you.

As you can see, it soon escalates – value each relationship and your unbeatable reputation can reap its rewards.

What can you offer a Partner or Affiliate?

To decide on a partner and make it work, you also need to consider…what can you offer a partner?

A key to this is to understand the potential partner's objectives – knowing what they want to achieve by working with you. Some will be purely motivated by revenue and therefore commissions they will earn will be their focus, while others might be looking for more than that.

1. Offer them commission or exchange

The number one consideration for any brand site promoting you is, what reward will they get in return?

For most this will be monetary. Therefore, what commission rates are you providing for each referred customer? Is it revenue share, CPA or CPC? Is it the most competitive rate in the market? What conditions will you be paying out, is it based on last click?

2. They might also want brand exposure

Partners aren't just considering a monetary or value return, they might want brand exposure instead.

Like-minded partners will want to seek mutual return of exposure on your site purely aiming at a branded return. If the exposure is not on your site, but rather a mutual event or joint product, then again the branding received will be important.

3. Or they want access to your customers

Aside from branding or commissions, partner brands might be looking for customers in return - they might want to see how many new customers they will get in return – if they promote you and you promote them to achieve customer acquisition.

Overall, we hope all of the above has given you food for thought on how to decide which partners to work with. As you can see there isn't really one answer, but many areas to consider. In conclusion though, we recommend choosing partners based on whether they will contribute to achieving your objectives.

Chapter 7: Why are Brand Partnerships are so lucrative yet so difficult for others? And how to succeed at them!

Brand Partnerships is a lucrative channel for most brands. It has been swept under the marketing rug and doesn't always get the recognition it deserves. But in recent years, it's slowly coming to the forefront, mainly thanks to the rise of digital tech and social media. The rise of Fintech, Proptech and Martech integrated partnerships, where one brand plugs into another, are becoming more and more popular through the advancement of API's. And co-branded campaigns are now far easier to create and advertise across the net.

One of the finest examples of this is where TripAdvisor partnered with Deliveroo and OpenTable by integrating their services into the TripAdvisor app. Another example being, StarlingBank and Moneybox teaming up to provide the money-rounding service all within the Starling platform. And lastly, Easyjet and Booking.com combining so you can book hotels directly through the Easyjet website.

Some brands though have found the process of partnering extremely difficult and struggled to replicate the above successes. So why is this? Here are 6 main reasons and how to mitigate them:

1. **Businesses should not get confused between *'Partnerships'* and *'Brand Partnerships'*** – at the same time don't get confused with these and buying media/advertising.

Everyone wants to use the buzzword *'partnership'* to describe their activity. I've seen bus-dev managers who send blanket messages on LinkedIn describing themselves as *Partnership Managers*, where in actual fact they are just trying to sell a tech/Saas platform. At the same time, Brand Partnerships are meant to be a long-term coming-together of two brands, whether it's integrations, interesting sponsorships, innovative attractions, a series of marketing campaigns, or utilising another brand as a reward mechanism. Plain and simple, it's not one brand buying advertising space on another brand's site or purchasing a payment or SaaS system to help you with operations. Here are some examples of what it should be – how it's not bus-dev nor media buying:

Chip & Emma – Integration Partnership

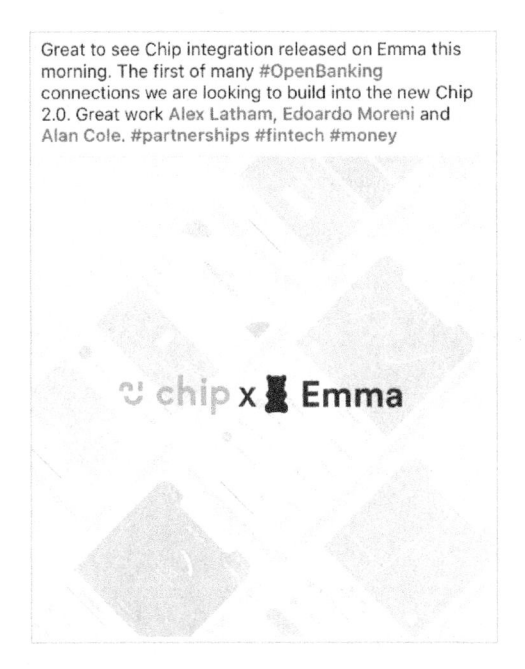

> Great to see Chip integration released on Emma this morning. The first of many #OpenBanking connections we are looking to build into the new Chip 2.0. Great work Alex Latham, Edoardo Moreni and Alan Cole. #partnerships #fintech #money

chip x Emma

Lastminute & HomeAway – Reward Partnership

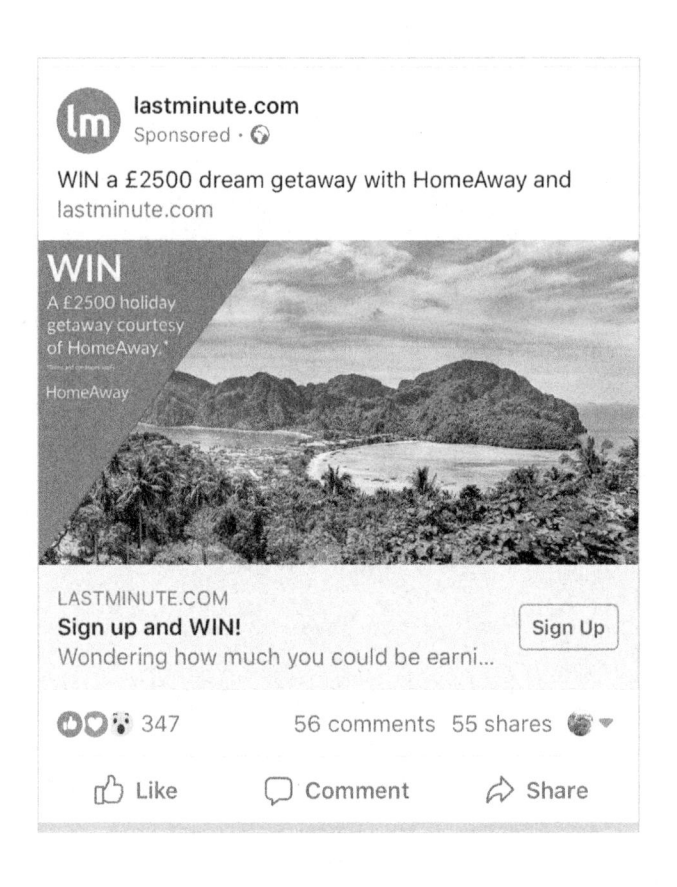

Airbnb & Le Louvre – Reward & Branding Partnership

> Exciting partnership with Le Louvre today to sleep under the glass pyramid and rediscover the museum through intimate concerts
>
> **Airbnb is giving people the chance to sleep under the iconic glass pyramid at the Louvre in Paris**
> businessinsider.com

2. **Do not be a short-termist** — many brands believe Brand Partnerships aren't successful because they are too short-termist. Businesses drive home the idea of partnerships and reach out to other brands to speed up acquisition and growth, but the reality is that not only do these agreements take months, if not years, to formulate, they are also a long-term growth tactic and shouldn't be seen as a one-off hit.

Don't get me wrong, a partnership campaign can take a few weeks to organise if you're lucky but it shouldn't be seen as a one off newsletter or marketing stunt. To really see the benefits you need to ensure that long-term commitment is made from both sides and you're both under the same pretence of time-frame and objectives.

Let's also mention the work that goes into partnerships, the processes in place is not about one off exposure – it includes finding your counterpart, discussing how to work together, commission negotiations, technical discussions, contracts, creative production and campaign analysis – all to consider.

3. **Everyone needs to be on-board** – this isn't a one-man channel. Companies wishing to partake in Brand Partnerships will hire an individual to arrange and run such campaigns. But it's not only about them, the entire company needs to have partnerships at the forefront of their strategy and priorities for it to be a success.

If not, what normally happens is that the marketing individual will onboard a huge brand name partner but the product team and engineers who might be required for the integration tell you they don't have capacity for another 6 months, or that there are other product developments which are more important.

So the lesson here is, partnerships needs to be backed by the board and bought-into by the entire cross-functioning team.

4. GDPR can be a bit of a problem — many brands lost a lot of email leads when GDPR was introduced (in Europe). It meant asking customers whether they wanted to be opted in for marketing, and many said no. From then on, we've had to ask customers if they are ok if we target them with third-party offers, and many also say no.

This poses a slight problem with partnerships. This led to brands not being 100% open about their customer base by sharing inflated figures to secure a deal.

My solution to this would be not to cover up, but be truthful how many customers are opted in, outline that your T&C's make it clear to customers whether they are opting in for third-party offers, meaning you're more likely to have a much more engaged customer base who actively wants to know about partners of yours.

5. **Finding a partnerships counterpart is not easy** — back to the earlier point, that we're seeing business-development managers call themselves 'partnership managers' and some brands are sp keen to run partnerships but not actually hire someone dedicated for the role.

This means it's not very easy to locate the individual who can make the Brand Partnership decisions — which for anyone in this role makes the process 10 times harder.

So, my recommended techniques are to message someone at the company you're trying to target with *'Can you introduce me to *the person responsible for your partnerships?'*. Either that or try to locate your counterpart with 'partnerships' in their title on LinkedIn to enquire about a partnership. These are two simple approaches that do work.

6. **Accept that some brands just aren't right for partnerships** — I've worked with a lot of brands that love the idea of this channel, understand the cost savings, efficiencies, brand exposure and PR benefits it brings, but when they come to run it, it simply doesn't work or they struggle to forge any long-lasting relationships.

The most common reason is their customer base. Some brands have highly engaged, loyal customers. Others have discreet customers who like their services but prefer to not be active. This leads to upselling and rewarding them becoming difficult. That means promoting or getting other brands to promote you, just simply won't work.

Others find they simply aren't well known enough yet for other brands to promote you. They want a name that their customers know, they want a product that can be trusted, or they want you to have a certain sized customer base. To these brands I say, there are other angles — try a monetary kick-back, try offering to pay for the integration or ask for a test campaign that's initially much smaller in approach.

Brand Partnerships are both lucrative and a challenge, but by understanding these 6 main reasons, brands can overcome the difficulties to succeed in this ever-growing marketing channel.

Chapter 8: How to analyse a Brand Partnership both online and offline

Choose your tracking

It's pivotal that we track campaigns effectively as we have two brands marketing under one campaign. Online we can use cookies and tracking codes implemented at different touch points along the user journey. Offline we can use codes, loyalty cards or purchase actions. When it comes to tracking you want to select a process that works for both partners:

- **Promo ID** – linked to your internal data or CRM.
- **Promo codes** – using codes such as 'TicketSale' or 'CheapTrains'.
- **Third-party tracking** – affiliate tracking, Adservers, Doubleclick.
- **UTM (Urchin Tracking Module)** – tracked via Google Analytics.

Analysing the campaign

Measuring results means gathering the data from your data-warehouse, Google Analytics, affiliate program, DTM (Dynamic Tag Manager) or Adserver. Once extracted you will need to slice and dice customer data to pull conclusions and illustrate the results accordingly.

Online

For digital marketers accurate analysis is the commandment of our industry, what makes our marketing unique over offline is that we can prove success. Using our tracking links and pulled data we can take the customer IDs and draw conclusions from their activity. Did the onsite integration, placement, social post, or newsletter attract the forecasted customer numbers for both sides? Did both achieve the CPAs (Cost per Action) they were aiming for at a positive ROI (Return on Investment)?

A good example of this is when I worked on a joint content campaign with Xero, an emerging accounting technology, we promoted their content via our communication channels and vice versa. Both embedded tracking links and analysed the number of customers clicking through. A very simple digital partnership that was effective at attracting each other's audience to our propositions.

Offline

Away from the devices it's a different kettle of fish. Any brand that advertises offline experiences the ongoing problem of tracking their outcome. Some popular solutions include; media value, promo codes or mobile data. Media value is an industry agreed figure allocating a value every time a logo was viewed, sometimes five times the spend. Channels such as PR tend to rely on such measurements. The problem is rather obvious, it's a fictional valuation and simply not good enough in today's digital age.

Mobile data is more interesting in that electronic billboards might in the future start to sync with our mobile activity using geolocation, tracking those who search for a brand after they have walked passed an ad's location. Again though it's based partially on assumptions.

A suggested way is to use a promo code where one can verbally, via receipts or loyalty cards take these into stores for additional benefits from a partner brand. It is most effective when overlapped with media value and location based data to provide a full picture for both brands to know when actions have been taken. It is also a great way of taking offline activity online, by entering the code via onsite checkout pages. I can't sugarcoat it though, we still don't have a clean answer but it can be done far more effectively than ever before and especially for partnerships.

Aside from acquisition or retention, brand impact can be measured through industry surveys or focus groups. Has the partner brand created an uplift in your popularity? Is your proposition now clearer due to being alongside a well-known brand?

Analysing the partnership

Aside from customer and brand impact the partnership itself can also be evaluated. Both sides should ask themselves whether the partnership was a success and whether to move forward with future projects or end collaborations. Such questions to ask are:

- How cooperative was the partner to work with?
- Did they ensure a stable relationship?

- Were full contractual terms met?
- Were payments made and creatives delivered on time?
- Did the partner brand work well with third party agencies?
- Was the partner brand useful in terms of knowledge sharing?
- Do both brands envisage running the campaign again?

Partner scorecard

Some brands like to rate a partner, especially if working with several at a time. Partners can be rated based on answers to certain questions, like the ones above, to determine a score. If the campaign analysis is then placed alongside these answers it can provide a useful picture of an entire partnership.

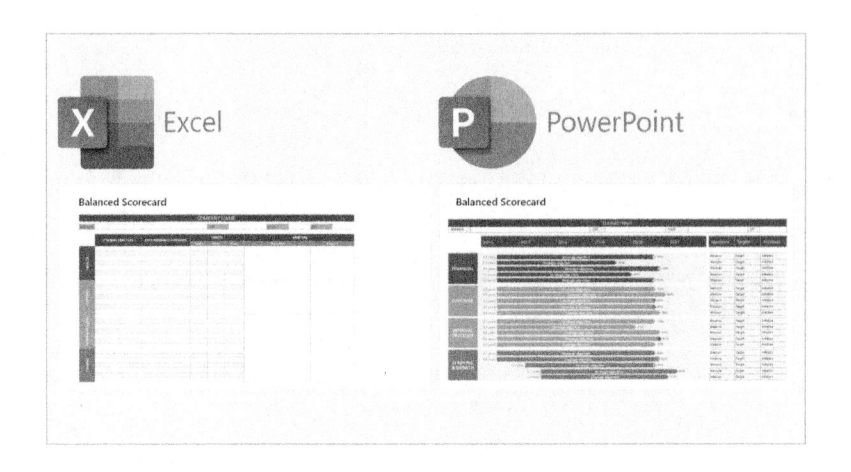

The campaign vs the partnership

There will be instances where a successful campaign can still mean a failed partnership and vice versa. It is possible for a highly profitable campaign to have been fraught with difficulties; an uncooperative unresponsive partner can mean a difficult partnership and one that you may not wish to run again.

On the contrary, a negative campaign with a positive partner means they're the right fit but there might be issues to overcome for future success.

Summary: The Future is ripe

With everything we have been discussing it makes sense to say that as digital and performance marketing expands so should Brand Partnerships. There is a direct correlation between increased digital marketing techniques, like Affiliation that we covered above, but also improved communication between brands, all contributing to the growth of partnerships.

As channels such social media continue to increase in popularity, everyone becomes more connected. Consumers talk to each other and new markets continue to open, in turn leading to increased competition as well as opportunity. With this being said, the need for collaboration will expand as brands fight to survive and capitalise.

All in all the future is ripe for the taking, for brands using any of the Brand Partnership techniques discussed in this book!

Thank you for reading this book & I hope you found it useful!

If you liked this content you can also...

1. *Follow us on* **LinkedIn @GrowPartnerships** *for the latest partnerships advice & insights*

2. *Take our popular Udemy courses:*

* *The Complete Guide to Partnership Marketing*

(100+ 5 star reviews & rated top 5% of all Udemy courses)

* [The Complete Guide to Affiliate Marketing](#)

(2k+ subscribers & 4.5/5 review score)

Disclaimer

The author takes no responsibility for any misuse of information contained in this book. All information has been taken from actual events and imagery or screenshots from free sources. If any owner or brand wishes to have any information removed, they may get in touch. He is not responsible for any copyright infringement as this is used purely for educational purposes and is happy to edit if required.

Printed in Great Britain
by Amazon